MONOLOGUES

ZILLE HUMA NAVID

AURAQ

Printed in the Islamic Republic of Pakistan.

Printed:	March, 2021
Edition:	1st
ISBN:	978-969-749-075-2
Cover Design:	Navid Akhtar Bajwa
Price:	Rs 800 PKR, $8 US

AURAQ
PUBLICATIONS

ISLAMABAD, PAKISTAN

raabta@auraqpublications.com | +92-300-0571-530
www.auraqpublications.com | @AuraqPublications

ISBN : 978-969-749-075-2

Printed and Bound by *Passive Printers* - www.passiveprinters.com

Dedicated to

those who introduced me to myself.

A GAME WITH NO RULES

Life is a weird game;

One can achieve everything that he has ever dreamed of,

And still can be unhappy.

MEMORIES

Good or bad,

You are my favorite memory.

THE UNNAMED

Most of the feelings are still unexplored,

Or maybe we forget to give them names.

A READER'S REPLY

A reader's reply to The Little Prince,

"We are always too young to know how to love."

TIME LIKES TO WRITE

Time never changes anyone;

It only fills in the blank parts of our personality.

A WRITER

I no longer urge a simple life;

My hardships give me strength to write.

WAIT FOR IT

Every single one of us is beautiful,

But not everyone is able to recognize it.

HOW STRONG IS YOUR LOVE?

If it is easy,

You will never know

The strength of your love.

A RECKONING

I cannot assure you

That people will not hurt you,

But what I do know is

That only people can mend your heart.

PETRICHOR

Rain heightens our emotions;

When we are happy, we find it refreshing,

And when we are sad, it brings woe and misery.

SADNESS IS PETER PAN

I wonder people celebrate sadness more than happiness;

Sadness is like a child who refuses to grow up and consistently needs pampering,

Whereas, happiness has become more independent with time.

ARTISTRY

I am in awe for humans' artistry,

How masterfully people flaunt their sanity

To conceal their insane self.

A FRIEND OF ALL SEASONS

There are books that can be read again and again.

A reader never gets saturated

If he builds an emotional connection to them;

The books become his true friends,

That always have something to say about a reader's growing experience.

These books know how to win your heart

With their most precious asset, words.

Only those who know the value of it

Can carry and display it rightly.

THE OPPRESSOR

Fate likes to practice power;

If we submit to its authority,

It might bring us our desired wish,

But if we rebel,

It makes us suffer.

LISTEN

There is a thing about silence;

It can be as loud as you want it to be.

UNDISCOVERED LANDS

I am fascinated by dreams;

Everyone seems happier there.

MYSTERIES OF LIFE

Life has its own ways:

Love is medicine, yet for some, it is a scar.

Love is a healer, yet for some, it is a wound.

Love is a blessing, and yet for some, it is a curse.

ENSLAVED BY THE TIME

Time is heartless;

It does not care about right or wrong

But what needs to be done,

Just like you.

BEAUTIFUL SCARS

We break,

To make space for new things.

THE GUARDIAN

Sometimes you have to trust fate for your own good,

Because it is only you, who have brought yourself to this stage

Where you cannot trust your own self with your own wellbeing.

THE PRISONER

Within the words, I am lost.

They imprisoned me, when I wanted to be free.

A CONTINUOUS WAR

In our urge to find happiness, we lose the peace.

Let us reverse our priority in the hope to find both.

WORDS AND MORE

Old books offer more stories than new ones;

A marked page,

An underlined passage,

A handwritten note,

Torn pages,

And a dry flower.

A CHOICE

If you choose love as a weapon,

I cannot assure you throne.

Love happens to be kind and compassionate.

SCARS

Memories are reliable,

They last longer than humans.

BLUE

A clear, vast sky; a calm lake,

Berries, bluebells, gemstones—

It is a color, she was told.

Feeling, it turned out to be,

Then meaningless became all the proofs.

HOME

In the hustle-bustle of the city,

If you can find a small corner of warmth,

Make it your home.

INNOCENCE

Once I was fascinated by a man's innocence,

He believed in perfect love.

A BEAUTIFUL MOSAIC

Don't be scared to break,

It gives you a unique texture.

It designs you to be more You.

ONE DAY

Be patient, my dear,

One day you will find someone,

Who will see you crystal clear,

With your perfections and imperfections,

And will still love you.

If you are smart enough,

You can make that one day right now.

THE TICKET

A word from him

Is my ticket to the past,

And my hope for the future.

COMPANION

To make an exceptional moment, one needs

A companion;

A person,

A book,

A pen,

A thought,

Or a dream.

FREE DELIVERIES

The worst things in life come in heavy packages with
free deliveries.

A FOOLISH PRINCESS

A naïve princess lets everything go uncontrollable,

Then cuddles the chaos that occupies every inch of her palace.

All the havoc, all the destruction,

Shattered artifacts into fragments,

Uncovered relics turning into monuments.

The princess still carriers a burden of hope,

One-day chaos will bring her peace.

A REMINDER

When a relation reminds you of painful memories more than good ones,

Let it go.

A FAILED ILLUSIONIST

I guess people inflict pain to know

How passionately they are loved by others.

But, what they do not know is that

Nobody wants to become a victim of someone's fascinations.

SIGNS

It was an unusual start,

And from that moment,

She believed something interesting was awaiting her.

MAYBE SOMEDAY

Maybe someday, I will have enough strength,

To pick up the broken pieces of my heart, and

To arrange them together and create a mosaic,

To cherish my heart and satisfy my soul.

EXPERIMENT

Let us exchange our roles this time,

And see where it leads.

TRUST ISSUES

It is pretty simple to believe a heart.

Mind—It is a clever place,

Beyond the reach.

MAKE PEACE

Accept it or not,

But fate is more stubborn than humans.

LOVE

When your heart cares for someone else's happiness
more than your own,

It is no longer yours.

SUBMISSION

Here,

I am sitting and thinking of a future,

Where your memories would not remind me of your
love,

But the reason of powerlessness to love again.

MENDING HEARTS

People

They hurt most of the time,

And in the remaining time,

They try to overcome the pain

That made them do so.

REMIX

Even music cannot understand me these days.

DREAMS

I live

Every moment,

Two times,

In real, and

When I imagine us,

Together.

THOUGHTS

You make the idea of love the loveliest.

THE PROPHECY

No matter how much you love,

You always end up hurting someone,

And it does not exclude you.

AN AMATEUR

I am not sure what I will write,

But what I do know is that,

Most of it will be about you.

THE EXPERTS

Humans are the cruelest creatures,

That exactly know what hurts the most.

BREATHING WORDS

Words become alive,

After you experience them.

REMAKE

No story is new!

All the stories are remake and mashup of previous stories;

Some find a resolution,

Whereas, most end in catastrophe and live longer.

THE PATTERNS

Life is uncertain,

Leading us to unfold our own realities.

FALLING

When one says 'we' instead of 'I',

Hoping he would not mind how you think about him.

GAMBLING

Life is a complex business;

When it is not challenging, it is boring.

THE LITTLE ARTISTS

Humans are pretty artistic,

In turning simple to complex.

THE INDEPENDENTS

Nobody wants to be saved;

All they want is to abide by their own rules.

FADING COLORS

Waiting is a painful process.

It consists of doubts, uncertainties, fear, anxiety,

And hope that fades with every passing moment.

LIVING DEAD

I have a rebellious urge to express myself through writing,

But my introvert nature paralyzes my hands,

Turning me into a living dead.

BLESSINGS

Isn't it beautiful,

How everyone defines and expresses love in their own beautiful, unique way?

But still, it is understood and embraced by others.

A LONG DAY

You are not around,

And it is going to be a long day.

A CELEBRATION

Every time we come across,

The stars, moon, flowers, and air

Celebrate our presence

Our togetherness.

MY SWEET LIES

When I say exactly the opposite of how I feel,

Forgetting, you understand unspoken words better.

PRESENTS FOR MY LONELY DAYS

Having a good memory is both

A blessing and a curse.

I can exactly recall how you made me feel.

THE SECRET ELEMENT

From the moment I saw you,

You have been my favorite constituent of the imagination.

BRAVE SOULS

Life always has a different plan from yours.

Some of us accept the challenge;

And rest, compromise.

MONOLOGUES

When dialogues end,

Monologues begin.

DO NOT LET GO

Staying together is not making anything better,

But still it gives a hope that together we can fight

The strangers inside us.

HABITS

People become a part of your life, willingly or
unwillingly.

When we get used to having them around, they
leave.

Sometimes life happens and sometimes a choice is
made.

LIFE; A CELEBRATION

I don't want you to be a part of my memories.

I want you to be an equal part of my life,

So that we can make new memories,

And cherish the old ones.

MY FINDINGS

Thank you and sorry are more feelings than words.

A SPELL

I can't overcome my fears.

They are bound to me as a spell.

I could not utter a word to make her better.

She was helpless,

And I was powerless.

CHANGING TIMES

Time is consistently changing,

And that is a fact.

It is only humans

Who give it a character of unpredictability.

THE FEAST

Writing is celebration.

A writer invites people to accompany him.

And together they set off on a journey,

In which they learn, explore, and create

Something beautiful and everlasting.

THE MEDALS

Sometimes I wonder how easily we are forgotten by those,

Who make a permanent mark on our memories.

SPECTRUM

A little more or less to anything makes it a new whole,

Words are reactive,

Hope x Infinity = Illusion,

Dislike x Infinity = Hate,

Attention x Infinity = Obsession,

Like x Infinity = Love,

Unhappy x Infinity = Sadness,

Surprise x Infinity = Miracle

SUFFERING

May be I enjoy it.

May be I like to suffer.

DAYDREAMING

You are not helping at all.

With you around me,

I cannot concentrate,

And your absence makes me lose all my senses.

PRESENT

Some days are just fine,

I keep myself busy and forget to notice the
movement of time.

Then there are the days that refuse to pass by,

And I think about you and memories of our time
together.

THE COLORS

Fate is like a drop of black paint,

Only a drop is enough to bring a massive change.

Struggle is like white paint,

Sometime, several drops are not enough to bring a noticeable difference.

THE ROUND CHARACTERS

Some stories do not need a villain to turn them around,

At times, the protagonist is enough.

A SINGLE THOUGHT

There are days when I feel happy;

I paint, I read, I listen music,

And then a single thought

Takes everything away.

ACCEPTANCE

There are the things that I like,

There are things that I love,

There are things that I know.

You are a stranger to me,

And I know I do not want it any different,

From the way it is now.

THE INVISIBLE BACKPACK

She has heard it from elders,

That your present depicts your future.

It happened quite often,

Worrying about future ruined her present.

God bless the memories of her past,

They feed her through hopeless days.

The memories were a reminder of her strength,

A gift from God that never ran out with time.

THE COMPLICATED

Loving him was never easy,

And he made it even more complicated.

THE LIST

Usually I am very sure of my wants.

But these days, I am more sure of the things I do not want,

And strangely your name comes to my mind without any effort.

DREAMS

The best thing about dreams is,

They are not expensive but precious.

THE MIST

If you truly love someone,

Then you can overcome any fear.

But if you are unable to overcome your fears,

Then probably your love and illusion are the same thing.

CLUELESS

I have no idea what will happen next.

It is like getting freedom after years of wait,

With uncertainties surrounding you.

It happens when you leave a story and enter a new one,

Completely clueless of the events and your own role.

A PATIENT STAR

She does not want to be unique and beautiful like
the moon,

Or powerful and bright like the sun.

She wants to be ordinary, a good ordinary—a star.

A star that hardly gets attention of people around.

It shines not for the sake of getting praises,

But for it knows this is how they fit in the universe.

And by chance if someone acknowledges it,

It is the reward for the patience and modesty.

The star never stops shining for the one who
appreciates

The beauty that was long forgotten.

NEON LIGHTS

The first time I noticed you,

I sensed

Loyalty,

Disloyalty,

Happiness,

Sadness,

Peace,

And anxiety.

But still you stood out.

FREEDOM

Write it down,

And

Be free.

THE MAGICIANS

I wonder, how can a person make you feel so desired?

And how can the same person make you feel so lonely?

THE LITTLE STEPS

Hold on! You might find something on the way.

It can be a grain of sand or a beach.

It depends what you crave more.

NO PLAN B

When it comes to love,

There are no options or shortcuts.

It is just one path with all that you have to offer.

A STUBBORN GIRL

She is not ready to make peace with her reality.

She is not ready to compromise on her dreams.

ONE MORE CHAPTER

Don't let your story end in tragedy;

And if it does, write another chapter,

Write a sequel.

AN OATH

When it comes to him,

She has no plan B.

A PERPETRATOR

I feel guilty when I forget you,

As if I am making a crime.

THE FAITH

With you by my side,

I never hesitate to live.

MR. PERFECT

First, they make you believe

They are your Mr. Perfect.

And later, they reveal their true colors.

ONE GLANCE

One glance,

And my whole world becomes colorful.

BREAK FREE

Hold on! You might find something beautiful on the next step.

Approach it, and do not let the previous captivate you,

To celebrate the sunshine of the coming future.

SELF-CARE

The moment I stopped loving you,

I fell in love with myself.

THE PASSION

I have felt your absence,

More passionately than your presence.

THE PAST

You are my nostalgic feeling,

My longing, my memory,

A home that once belonged to me.

A LESSON

Your love is no more a memory,

But a Lesson.

A COMPARISION

I love his memories more than

I love him.

TWISTED THOUGHTS

There are as many interpretations of the world

As its inhabited beings.

Yet we can't figure out ours properly.

THE DISGUISED

I showed you my dreams,

I welcomed you to my world,

And you shattered it,

And turned it into a real world.

LOST

Your thoughts do not excite me anymore.

Is it because I overthink about you?

Or

Is it that I have lost interest in you?

THE ART OF SHARING

Those, who do not know the art of sharing,

Shed tears.

A FORMULA

Balance is no good for me,

Calculated outcome never excites me.

Formulate your own formula,

Own your world.

A SKY FULL OF STARS

So many dreams,

So many wishes,

So many prayers,

Linked to one being.

HANDMADE

We make things complex,

And then take pleasure in resolving them.

AN UNTOLD STORY

The tragedy of mankind is that

They do not enjoy the process,

Neither do they embrace the moment

They struggled for.

THE KEY

Most of us submit ourselves to the most powerless.

And some of us are destroyed by them.

A WISH THAT WAS GRANTED

Her goal was not to find recognition.

A few connected to her,

And she was happy in her small community.

TEMPTATIONS

Evil is easily recognizable;

Pretty common,

But still most of us are tempted by it.

THE STORIES AND US

There are so many stories that we are a part of,

Some as a character, few as a reader, and

If we are strong enough, then as a writer.

I wonder how different narratives shape us, mold us,

And link us all together.

IS THIS WORTH IT?

The most anticipated moments,

Disappoint you the most.

ALIENATED

There are no parallels between dreams and reality.

If dreams turn to reality exactly the way we anticipate,

Still it won't bring us the desired charm.

At times, nothing works, not dreams nor reality.

A SMALL TALE

Why do you always seem so sad?

Because it suits me.

What do you mean?

I feel more comfortable being sad.

It's something that I have known for a while now;

Whereas, happiness is still a stranger to me.

WELCOME

Be humble,

Let them accompany you.

A SOUL AS VAST AS SEA

Her soul is as vast as sea;

With its own aroma, beauty, and fierceness,

Her presence can be touched by those who are close to her,

And felt by those, who crave for signs of hope.

She was beyond anyone's control.

Her presence can only be cherished

And celebrated by being a part of it.

HOLDING ON

When you are about to give up,

Stay put, that is when you are nearest to your achievement.

REWINDING

At times, I wish to give up everything

That I have so far,

So that I struggle to recollect them

And to value them more.

KNOCK KNOCK!

And again, emptiness is knocking at my door.

Neither I am able to bring light in anyone's life,

Nor anyone can bring it in my life.

As if the whole world is covered with a dark shadow,

As if angels left the world,

And I cannot wait to leave it too.

TURNING TABLES

When they like something, they want to possess it.

They are incapable of accepting something
noteworthy

Not a part of their life.

They wear those gems believing it makes them
valuable,

Whereas, they only become crueler, beastly and
nastier,

Everything opposite of glorious.

ACHE

Shun writing,

Everything is expressed already,

And what is not expressed,

We suffer through it.

WEIRD YET BEAUTIFUL

We are different yet alike.

We make rules and break them.

We love, and yet, we are capable of hate.

We are so stubborn yet so flexible.

We love laughing yet we cry often.

We are made noble but prone to evil.

We are equipped with knowledge but still ignorant.

We kill each other yet we are scared of death.

We are unsure yet we call ourselves believers.

We hope but still we live in doubts.

We try knowing we will never be perfect.

Humans, we are weird yet beautiful.

THE CONSENT

I feel more connected to your absence,

It stays longer,

And never leaves me without my consent.

A GUEST

Hey! Welcome back, lonely days,

Like always, you arrived like an unexpected guest,

And like always, I am going to serve you

With tears, memories, and lots of sleep.

PAYBACK

Sometimes, we choose the words,

And

Sometimes, words choose us.

ACKNOWLEDGEMENT

Light is truly recognized by those,

Who have known the darkness.

DISENTANGLE

It is never a bad idea to come back home,

To sit back and relax,

To feel your roots,

To know how far you are,

To connect to your past,

To build the bridge to the present,

To feel less lonely,

And to know yourself better.

PEOPLE

There are only three kinds of people in this world,

Those who celebrate sadness,

Those who celebrate happiness, and

Those who celebrate life.

GRAY

It looked balanced,

But was recognized as different,

It was repelled by both,

Even though it was consisting of both.

They blamed it for not being one of them,

Whereas, it was nothing but natural.

A SHORT POEM

Happiness spreads,

Sadness penetrates.

THE MASS

When you lose somebody,

But cling to the things

That hold sentimental value

In hope to have a small piece of that person.

COMMITTED

This time, she was standing for the words

She once said to him, not for

The feelings she had for him.

A LOST TREASURE

Of all the treasures that I had,

I miss you the most.

NUMB

I have become so numb with pain

That I want to cry so bad,

But tears don't know the dead.

ILLUSIONIST/ POSITIVIST

Indeed, she was a strange girl.

She wanted to paint a bright picture of the world,

From all the faded colors she was offered.

FINE LINES

When it comes to choice,

We are always given black and white,

With no grays.

DISTANCE

There is beauty in everything.

Distance brings its own flavor to relations,

Like a waterfall that sprinkles its sweet droplets,

A sun hidden in clouds that cannot stop shining,

A lighthouse that revives the hope,

Sleeping in hope to see the sunrise.

UNTAMED HABITS

She is bad with timings.

She worries about chaos before it approaches her.

When chaos reaches her, she wonders.

When there is peace, she worries about the chaos

That might or might not knock at her door.

A FORGOTTEN MAGICIAN

With time, happiness has become a rare trait in a world full of sorrows.

Whereas, sadness has become an expensive lifestyle.

People sacrifice everything to find the magician,

So it grants them the most expensive ticket to visit the world of sadness.

THE UNSAID

I am fascinated by all

That is not communicated.

FOOLISH BEINGS

There is no right person for anyone,

These are all illusions,

That make us even more unhappy.

We set standards and demand from others to meet them.

Come on, you foolish being!

It's not always about you.

REVENGE

Revenge never brings peace.

It merely satisfies ego.

PROMISE ME NO PROMISES

If you trust him,

Then why do you seek promises?

If promises are guarantee,

Then why do words and actions contradict?

Let it go.

You cannot control it.

Embrace what you have.

How you can ask for sureties,

When you are not certain about yourself.

LIVE IT

The meaning of life does not lie in knowing it,

But living it.

HOME

You cannot protect me,

Not from this world,

It is my home.

Sooner or later,

I have to face it.

AN INTIMITATION

It is better not to have it

Than to have it,

And let it go.

A THINKING BEING

No matter how much positivity a person holds,

He always feels,

And these feelings make him think, think a lot.

SIMPLICITY

I do not want to be all consumed by my passion;

A little simplicity always fascinated me.

WHO'S TO BLAME?

I live in a world where people set out to gain happiness, and end up chasing sadness.

It has nothing to do with anyone but their intrigued nature.

LIMITLESS

Silence goes there,

Where words can't reach.

THE INVISIBLE WOMAN

She feels everything,

But there is no one to understand her, not anymore.

Sooner or later, everyone becomes a victim of their own tragedies,

That they think the pain she endures is nothing but a scratch.

AN OLD SONG

He is like an old song in her playlist.

This was the fourth time she fell in love with him with her beating heart.

He has a deep connection with her soul, as if the song perfectly suits her needs.

She confines to it and defines herself through it.

HOPE

It is a consistent companion in all shades of life.

Whether it gets acknowledged or not, still it does not leave your side.

In our stubbornness, we refuse to recognize it, but it keeps on smiling with no malice.

Hope does not know the art of giving up on humans.

THE BELIEF

Nobody believes in you.

Everyone believes in themselves.

FATE

They are manipulative.

They find it difficult to trust each other, and at times, even themselves.

So I don't bother when they seek my help.

They never understand my job description because none of them can qualify for it.

They are all about themselves; if it satisfies them, then let it be.

They create mess and then blame me for it.

When everything goes uncontrollable, they look at me as if I am the God.

They let me have the authority, and I don't mind it.

They are indeed the most ignorant for being unaware of their capabilities.

Here is a secret, not only you can write your own destiny, But also you can alter mine.

THE UNIDENTIFIED

The strangest thing is that most of us meet happiness as a stranger.

We do not recognize its presence until it is long gone.

A WILD CARD

Need a wild card in the moments of intense despair?

Recognize your distinct strength to step up your game.

HURRICANE

I am at loss.

I want to step back.

I am uncertain about my capabilities.

I only have a sense about it, and

It fills my mind with unrest.

JAILBIRDS

We are all prisoners and will always be.

It just depends on how far we build the wall.

A few walls appear so massive to demolish,

Whereas a few appear small,

And that's how we enjoy our so called freedom.